Dreams
and
Visions

Illustrations by
Paul Blake

ISBN 0 947338 79 9

This edition published 1996 exclusively for Selecta Book Ltd,
Folly Road, Roundway, Devizes, Wiltshire, UK.

Dreams
and
Visions

We need time to
dream,
time to remember,
and time to reach the
infinite.
Time to be.

GLADYS TABER

Almost suspended,
we are laid asleep in body,
and become a living soul:
While with an eye made quiet
by the power of harmony,
and the deep power of joy,
We see into the life of things

WILLIAM WORDSWORTH

We see sleeping
what we
wish for waking.

GEORGE PETTIE

Many's the long night
I've dreamed of cheese-
toasted, mostly.

ROBERT LOUIS STEVENSON

If I awake
surrounded by flowers,
I can hardly remember
my sad dreams.

TRADITIONAL SPANISH SONG

There was a time when meadow,
grove, and stream
The earth, and every
common sight,
To me did seem
Apparelled in celestial light,
The glory
and the freshness
of a dream.

WILLIAM WORDSWORTH

Nowhere can man find
a quieter or more
untroubled retreat
than in his own soul.

MARCUS AURELIUS

If you can remember
dreams of flying and
soaring like a bird,
or dancing, or singing
more perfectly
than you ever thought
possible,
you know that no
second-hand account
of such events
could ever give
you
the thrill you felt
in the dream.

GAYLE DELANEY

Sleep is often the only
occasion in which man cannot
silence his conscience;
but the tragedy of it is that
when we do hear our
conscience speak in sleep,
we cannot act, and that,
when able to act,
we forget what
we knew in our dream.

ERICH FROMM

Dreaming permits
each and every one of us
to be quietly
and safely insane
every night of our lives.

WILLIAM DEMENT

I am interested in
the effect dreams may have
upon our lives.
I do not care
much about
what my living does
to my dreams,
but I would like to know
how my dreaming shapes
(if it does)
my life.

JESSAMYN WEST

One of the most adventurous
things left us
is to go to bed.
For no one can lay a hand
on our dreams.

E. V. LUCAS

I would rather think of life
as a good book.
The further you get into it,
the more it begins to come
together and make sense.

RABBI HAROLD KUSHNER

Our truest life
is when we
are in dreams
awake.

HENRY DAVID THOREAU

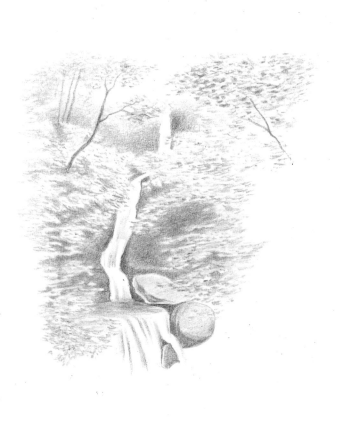

You must have chaos
in your heart
to give birth
to a dancing star.

FRIEDRICH NIETZSCHE

Are we then God's dream
set to music
in the place where the sea
and the wind have
begun to awake
and think?

GUY MURCHIE

Dreams take us
to levels
that we would otherwise
be afraid to strive for.

BILL BEHAM

Nothing said to us,
nothing we can learn
from others,
reaches us so deep
as that which we find in
ourselves.

THEODORE REIK

Dreams surely are for the
spirit
what sleep is for the
body.

FRIEDRICH HEBBEL

No man can reveal to you aught
but that which already lies
half asleep in the dawning
of your knowledge.

KAHLIL GIBRAN

I dreamt I dwelt in marble halls,
  And each damp thing
  that creeps and crawls
  Went wobble-wobble
    on the walls.

LEWIS CARROLL

By lessons some are
enlightened,
By sleep
others are inspired.

SIBYLLINE ORACLES

It is easy to forget
that it was dreams
that led you
to where you are now.

BILL BEHAM

Existence
would be intolerable
if we were never to
dream.

ANATOLE FRANCE

Learn
from your dreams
what you lack.

W.H. AUDEN

Children
love to be alone
because alone is where
they know themselves,
and where they dream.

ROGER ROSENBLATT

I don't know whether
I was then a man dreaming
I was a butterfly,
or whether
I am now a butterfly
dreaming I am a man.

CHUANG TZU